YOUR KNOWLEDGE

Imprint:

Copyright © 2011 GRIN Verlag
Print and binding: Books on Demand GmbH, Norderstedt Germany
ISBN: 9783656109815

This book at GRIN:

https://www.grin.com/document/187599

A. Glatz

African American Vernacular English in Contemporary Music

A linguistic analysis

GRIN Verlag

GRIN - Your knowledge has value

Since its foundation in 1998, GRIN has specialized in publishing academic texts by students, college teachers and other academics as e-book and printed book. The website www.grin.com is an ideal platform for presenting term papers, final papers, scientific essays, dissertations and specialist books.

Visit us on the internet:

http://www.grin.com/

http://www.facebook.com/grincom

http://www.twitter.com/grin_com

Justus-Liebig-Universität Gießen

Institut für Anglistik

Bachelor Thesis

SoSe 2011

African American Vernacular English in
Contemporary Music: a Linguistic Analysis

Date: September 7, 2011

Table of Contents

List of Tables

1. Introduction

This thesis investigates the use of African American Vernacular English in
contemporary music. AAVE is an ethnic variety spoken by many, though not all,
African Americans living in the United States. This dialect does not have one name
only, but is also called "Negro dialect," "Nonstandard Negro English," "Black
English," "Black Street Speech," "Black Vernacular English," "Black Vernacular
English," or "African American English." I would like to add that some terms are
historical. It is crucial to know that researchers call it differently because to a large
degree it depends on the time he/she conducted research on this topic. Today, the
dialect is either called African American Vernacular English or African American
English.

The words "contemporary music" in the title refer to Hip Hop. This music
genre was chosen to be investigated because out of the music genres African
Americans are involved in, it is the one that generates most of the sales and is the
most popular one. The rappers which are going to be analyzed in this thesis use many
of the features of the African American vernacular. Given the huge number of
AAVE features, only one of them will be analyzed, the copula verb *to be*, which in
the following will only be called "the copula." According to Wolfram, the copula is
"one of the most often described structures of AAVE" (2008: 517). For this reason,
the copula might be an interesting feature to look at. When researchers examined
AAVE in the past, they did not necessarily take music as a source of data, but rather
spoken language. One has to know that language in music is a different genre of
language use, which differs from the usual use of the language. Music can be
considered an artistic expression, but not "real" speech. Nevertheless, as music has
always been and presumably will always be a big part in African American culture, it
should be possible to recognize features of AAVE and use music as a reliable source.
In the analysis conducted in this thesis, the use of the copula will be examined by
having a look at the lyrics of three famous rappers from the US: Tupac, Jay-Z and 50
Cent. Even though the three of them can be assigned to "gangsta rap", they all differ
from each other. They all started their careers in different decades, come from
different cities and have a different style of rapping. What they have in common is
that they are African American rappers from a lower class who grew up in poverty

1

and have become successful musicians. The similarities make it possible to compare the three of them and choose a representative corpus for Tupac, Jay-Z and 50 Cent for the analysis. The differences give rise to diachronic conclusions about their use of copula deletion as well, as they had their climax of success in different decades. This means that we can have a look at how the three rappers changed their use of copula deletion in the course of their careers. In the end, the analysis will show that there can be found similarities as well as differences between the rappers. We will see that Tupac and Jay-Z increased their use of copula deletion, whereas 50 Cent decreased it. We will also see that, on average, the rappers analyzed in this thesis have increased their use of copula deletion over the course of time (from their first to their last album).

At the end of the thesis, the question of whether Hip Hop music can be a reliable source of AAVE language will be answered. We will find out that Hip Hop music is not necessarily a good source because language in music is too creative and too dependent on rhythm.

2. Background Knowledge on AAVE

In the first part of the thesis, the theoretical background of AAVE is going to be specified. At first, it has to be made clear what AAVE is, where its origins lie and who its speakers are. Likewise, it is important to consider other issues linked to the current research status of AAVE, such as its role in the classroom or in professional settings, as well as attitudes of the general public towards it. In section 2.2. an overview about the most important phonological, grammatical and lexical features is given with a focus on the copula. In addition, the copula's origins and its development is going to be pointed out. Subsequently, Hip Hop music and its link to AAVE speakers is going to be discussed in 2.3. Finally, in 2.4 the research question of deletion of copula *be* in Tupac's, Jay-Z's and 50 Cent's lyrics is going to be explained.

2.1 Definition, Origin, Speakers of AAVE and Attitudes Towards It

In this section, an overview about important background knowledge about AAVE is given. Part of this section will be a definition of AAVE as well as the description of its potential speakers. Also, it is necessary to show where the origins of this dialect might be. Moreover, other research topics, such as how AAVE is treated in the classroom and professional settings, and attitudes towards it in the general public are dealt with in this section.

Green defines AAVE as follows: "African American English refers to a linguistic system of communication governed by well defined rules and used by some African Americans (though not all) across different geographical regions of the USA and across a full range of age groups" (Green 2004: 77). She makes clear AAVE has rules and consequently is a widely recognized system of speech that has syntactical independence. One of the most important information Green provides in this quotation is that AAVE is related to the ethnicity of its speakers. We deal with a "ethnic variety," which basically means that it consists of "linguistic features which reflect the regular interactions people have – those they talk to most often" (Holmes 2008: 184). In this quotation, Holmes assumes that people with e.g. the same ethnicity tend to have the most interactions with each other. The fact that AAVE is an ethnic variety should not be misunderstood. Not every American with African roots automatically speaks this variety, nor is it impossible that someone with European or other roots can adopt this dialect. It is often claimed that about 80 percent or more of all African Americans are able to speak this dialect. However, Rickford says that this is rather a "guesstimate" (Rickford 1999: 9) than a number that could be proved by serious studies. It is very hard to identify the speakers for two main reasons. The first one is that it is difficult to tell at which point you are a speaker of AAVE. It is not possible to say which of the many features of AAVE you have to use to be an ordinary speaker of this variety. The second reason refers to the fact that many African Americans use AAVE alongside Standard American English (SAE) or some regional standard. There might be speakers who exclusively speak the standard, even though they are able to use AAVE. Some of them might use both dialects, depending on the context of the speech situation, e.g. some might rather use AAVE when talking to someone with the same complexion while tending to SAE when talking to an European American (Rickford 1999: 10). Last but not least, there is a group that exclusively speaks AAVE, who are, by the way, often said to originate from lower classes. As we can see, there are difficulties in stating who is a AAVE speaker or not. Generally, one can say that such speakers often come from urban areas and use it in informal contexts. One also has to keep in mind that there might be variation by age and gender. The question of who the speakers of AAVE are is a major interest in current research.

Another interesting topic is the origin of AAVE. There is only a limited amount of data available on the early stages of the language of Africans in America, i.e. the language of slaves brought to the colonial United States and the following development of the language. For this reason, there is no definite answer that can be given on the origin of AAVE, but several hypotheses were offered by Wolfram and Schilling-Estes (2006), which I am going to present in the following section. The four hypotheses the authors name are *Anglicist Hypothesis*, *Creolist Hypothesis*, *Neo-Anglicist Hypothesis* and the *Substrate Hypothesis*.

The *Anglicist Hypothesis*, sometimes called *Dialectologist Hypothesis*, maintains that AAVE does not derive from African languages to any respect, but only from English spoken by European Americans. According to this theory, English was the main factor that influenced the language of Africans in America. During the time they were held in bondage as slaves, they were forced to interact with their masters and other white people from their local and regional area who were the ones in power. This is the reason why many slaveholders often tried to prevent the contact with other slaves on the plantations. Evidence for this theory is the fact that certain features of AAVE were also found in other American regional or social varieties, such as in the Southern dialect. Thus, the language of African Americans originates from SAE as a dialect.

The next hypothesis, the *Creolist Hypothesis*, states that today's AAVE developed from a creole language which emerged after Africans were brought to America. Before a creole can develop in a speech community, a pidgin has to be used first. Amberg and Vause define pidgin as "a language that arises when people who do not speak the same language come into contact" (2009: 155). As the language situation was quite difficult with English, Spanish, Dutch and Portuguese slave traders and African slaves, they had to develop a way of communication to understand each other. This was how the pidgin was "born". If speakers of a pidgin have children and these children continue to speak this language and develop further grammatical and other linguistic features, we are talking of a creole, which can be seen as a full-fledged new language. The evidence for the *Creolist Hypothesis* lies in the fact that today's AAVE has several similarities with some of the Caribbean creole languages. If we think about AAVE for a moment, we realize quite quickly that today it rather resembles SAE than an assumed creole. Wolfram & Schilling-Estes explain this development of the former creole by referring to a process called *decreolization*, which is described as follows: "In this process, creole structures are lost or replaced by non-creole features. Decreolization, however, was gradual and not necessarily complete, so that the vestiges of its creole predecessor may still be present in modern AAE" (Wolfram 2006: 221). According to them, the former creole adopted almost all features from SAE and only some features of the creole remained, such as the copula *be* absence, which is dealt with in this paper later on.

Coming to the next hypothesis about the origin of AAVE, it is important to know that in the 1970s and 1980s, a lot of new data on the language of African Americans emerged and showed that their language was much more similar to European American English than assumed before. Linguists started to doubt that

AAVE had its origin in a presumed creole. For this reason, the *Neo-Anglicist Hypothesis* emerged. It maintains that present AAVE is "directly linked to the early British dialects brought to North America" (Wolfram 2006: 222), and since then the language diverged so much that you are hardly able to reconstruct the original language. Labov asserts that "the general conclusion that is emerging from studies of the history of AAVE is that many important features of the modern dialect are creations of the twentieth century and not an inheritance of the nineteenth" (Labov 1998: 119). Thus, AAVE diverged from SAE "on its own" because its speakers established new linguistic features.

However, there was not much support for this theory, so that Wolfgang & Schilling-Estes introduced the *Substrate Hypothesis*, which maintains that enduring differences between AAVE and European American English have always existed, even though there might have been some features that AAVE incorporated from regional dialects. This hypothesis states the two dialects have influenced each other in so far that *substrates* such as inflectional *–s* absence or copula absence came into being. This constellation of two languages influencing each other so much that the differences between the two endure beyond the original contact circumstance, Wolfgang & Schilling-Estes call a *substrate effect* (cf. Wolfgang 2006: 223). Thus, the early contact between the dialects is responsible for today's differences. In comparison with the *Anglicist* or *Neo-Anglicist Hypotheses*, the *Substrate Hypothesis* does not claim that earlier AAVE and European American English were identical.

Though researchers were able to find evidence for all of the above hypotheses, no clear answer about the origin of AAVE can be given. Given the limitations of data, a final answer seems to be impossible. For now, one has to accept the fact that there are only hypotheses trying to explain the origins of AAVE.

Another controversial topic on AAVE is the attitude towards it in educational or professional settings. As Rickford states, speakers of AAVE need a certain proficiency in SAE in order to become successful in the Unites States (cf. Rickford 1999). A big problem is that too many African American students have very poor reading skills and a low academic achievement in general. The issue is that Standard English is required in all professions and seems to be the most accurate form to talk when being at work (cf. Green 2002: 223). Attitudes in professional settings are very negative towards AAVE, but to other non-standard dialects as well. If AAVE is heard by co-workers or employers in professional settings, the speaker is often perceived as someone with low communication skills because she/he is unable to communicate in the appropriate way. The general public often perceives AAVE as unintelligible speech not to be taken seriously as a dialect on its own. For this reasons, researchers such as Lisa Green demand an adjustment of African Americans to the linguistic requirements at work:

> employees have the obligation to speak what the employer deems appropriate for the company, and the employer has the power to demand a particular variety of language. The message is that AAE [African American English] is not appropriate language for use in a professional setting. (Green 2002: 223)

According to Green, employees speaking AAVE should not insist on speaking their speaking their dialect, but rather adjust to the norms set on the workplace. As dialects in general are often evaluated negatively, speakers should try to speak SAE without being offended that they are not allowed to speak however they want. The same counts for the use of AAVE in the classroom. In many cases the teacher's negative attitude towards AAVE can discourage a student's will to learn SAE. If a teacher has a negative attitude towards a dialect (which could be any dialect in this case, not only AAVE), he might already have low expectations for this student. If the teacher then puts the student into special language courses to get rid of her dialect, this rejection towards the student's dialect might cause the student to be offended and to become demotivated. For this reason it is often hard for AAVE speakers to learn SAE. Another reason might be that they often interact with people speaking the same dialect. Consequently, they might lack practice in SAE and are not able to overcome the differences between AAVE and SAE. Because of the fact that society wants them to speak SAE in official situations, some AAVE speakers might have a very bad motivation, thinking that SAE is a characteristic of the majority, i.e. white people. The fact that they interact mostly with people speaking the same dialect and identifying the most with them lead to a negative perception towards SAE.

2.2 Overview of the Most Important Features of AAVE

In this section, I will give an overview of the most important phonological, grammatical and lexical features of AAVE in comparison to SAE as presented by

Tottie (2002) and Rickford (1999). I will first introduce a few of the phonological features of AAVE.

The largest differences with regard to phonology can be found in the consonant system. One prominent feature of AAVE is that it is non-rhotic, which basically means that the letter *r* is not pronounced in certain contexts. Besides the word-final *r* (as in the word *letter*), it is also possible to leave out an intervocalic *r*, i.e. an *r* between two vowels (e.g. *barrel*, which then sounds like [bæl]). Other features are the realization of final velar *ng* as alveolar *n*, such as in *singin'* for SAE *singing*), and the "reduction of word-final clusters in words like test, desk, hand, build, child are frequent, so that they sound like tess, dess etc." (Tottie 2008: 220). Another interesting feature is the devoicing of word-final voiced stops after a vowel, i.e. the realization of [d] as [t], such as in *bad*, which becomes [bæt] or [k] for [g], as in [pɪk] for *pig*.

The grammar of AAVE differs the most from SAE and is the most noticeable one if you listen to AAVE speakers. The verb phrase is probably the most prominent aspect of the grammar with regard to AAVE. According to Tottie, AAVE "has more possibilities of indicating for instance whether an event or action is ongoing, habitual or repeated, recently finished, or finished in the remote past" (Tottie 2008: 221) than other varieties of English. AAVE speakers use an invariant form of the verb *be* to indicate that an action is habitual. An example for this is the sentence *Lisa be mad*, which basically means "Lisa is always mad". Another feature is the use of stressed *been*, spelled BIN, which refers to the fact that an action started a long time ago in the past and is still going on. Rickford uses the example "She BIN married", meaning "She has been married for a long time (and still is)" (Rickford 1999: 6). In case AAVE speakers want to express future meaning, they use the word *will*, but because of *l*-deletion (*l* is sometimes vocalized in the end of words) it often sounds as if *will* is not used. Thus, "He'll miss you tomorrow" sounds as "He miss you tomorrow" (Tottie 2002: 223). People who are not familiar with this variety aspect might assume that AAVE speakers simply leave out *will*. The form *will have* is expressed by substituting *will have* with *be done* as in the following example by Rickford: "She *be done* had her baby" instead of "She *will have* had her baby"

8

(Rickford 1999: 6). The third person singular is often not indicated in AAVE, i.e. *-s* is simply left out: "He sing" instead of "He sings".

Negation is special as AAVE speakers use the expression *ain't* as a generalized negator. *Ain't* can substitute "am not", "is not", "are not", "has not", "have not" and " did not". For instance, it is possible to use ain't in both sentences "He *ain'* here" and "He *ain'* do it", although *ain't* signifies "is not" in the first example and "did not" in the second. Also note that *ain't* is often pronounced as *ain'*. Beside this, AAVE has a feature called *double or multiple negation*, which means that there are two or more words that express negation but do not cause a change in meaning. In a related fashion, "*nothing* and *no* are used instead of the standard forms *anything* or *any*, as in "I *ain't* got *no* car" for "I don't have a car". Tottie quotes a sentence, in which we find four (!) negatives: "*Ain't no* cat *can't* get in *no* coop", meaning "There is no cat that can get into any cage" (Tottie 2002: 224).

The last grammatical feature I would like to describe is the most significant one for this paper: the absence of copula/auxiliary *is* and *are* for present tense states and actions, as in the following example: *He happy.* It is important to mention that the absence of *to be* almost never occurs in the first person singular, i.e. *am.* The copula is one of the most studied features in the course of AAVE studies and therefore an interesting one to look at when it comes to music as there has not been a lot of research so far. As the copula absence is the linguistic item to be analyzed later in this thesis, we should have a closer look on the historical and current development of this feature. Dialectologists and creolists oppose each other when talking about the origins of the AAVE pattern of copula deletion usage. The crucial question is the following one: "Do speakers have *is* as an underlying aspect of their dialect, or does the vernacular have a vacuous (that is Ø) form that gradually gives way to the intrusion of *is* as speakers gain more exposure to standard English?" (Baugh 1983: 19). Dialectologists maintain that AAVE speakers actually have in mind that the copula is used in certain positions and that a natural process in the development of the AAVE dialect caused the absence. Creolists, on the contrary, are of the opinion that the null copula derived from English-based creoles and pidgins that were spoken in the African diaspora. As speakers had to deal more and more with the English language proper and its copula use, speakers adopted this feature in some cases as part of decreolization. However, AAVE speakers still leave out the feature in some positions. All in all, it is quite well possible that several causes led to the development of copula absence in AAVE. Winford asserts the following about its source: "the copula pattern of AAVE is best explained as the result of imperfect second language learning, with transfer from creolized or restructured varieties playing a significant role. In other words, multiple causation was at work here" (Winford 1998: 111). Instead of assigning the source of AAVE to one of the two opposing views, Wolfram and Thomas state that the explanation might be a combination of the two of them.

Another copula-specific issue is that it is sometimes left out by European Americans as well. So, copula deletion is a feature that can also be assigned to SAE. Wolfram and Schilling-Estes present the current research status on copula deletion in the South of the US compared to AAVE in one chapter of their work "American English." They state that "neither European American nor African American speakers delete the copula when the form is *am*" (Wolfram 2006: 215). This means that *is* and *are* are the only cases where *be* is deleted from speech. Moreover, the deletion of *are* is the most common one in both dialects, but it is far more frequent in AAVE (Wolfram 2006: 215). As a last point, the two authors say that when the copula is followed by *gonna*, both speech communities delete *is* (e.g. *She gonna do it*), but European American do not delete *is* very often when other words than *gonna* follow it (less than 5 percent). African Americans, on the contrary, show high levels of frequency (e.g. *She crazy*) (Wolfram 2006: 216).

Coming back to the most important features of AAVE, the vocabulary "is less distinctive than its grammar and phonology, but it has certainly added much to American English" (Tottie 2002: 225). There are some expressions which are modified in AAVE, so that they acquire a new meaning. An example is the word *cool*, which means "excellent" among other things and originally came from AAVE. Nowadays, it is an established expression in SAE that everybody uses. The word *bad* has the meaning "very good" in AAVE and *uptight* has the meaning of "tense, anxious". Another feature of the vocabulary is the expression *call oneself*, meaning "claim, pretend" in SAE, such as in "He calls himself a cook", which basically wants to tell us that the person thinks she/he is a cook, but in fact does not cook very well.

2.3 Hip Hop and AAVE

In this section, we have a look at Hip Hop and its relationship to AAVE. It is crucial to know what Hip Hop really is and where it originated from, before coming to its cultural and linguistic relationship to AAVE. As Hip Hop has its own language, it is necessary to have knowledge about in how far it is similar to AAVE.

To begin with, it needs to be clarified what Hip Hop is and what its relationship to rap is, as people often tend to interchange the two words. First of all, Hip Hop is not a music style, but a culture consisting of four subcultures: MCing (rapping), DJing (turntablism), breakdancing and graffiti art (spraying). Accordingly, rap as a music style is part of Hip Hop. Furthermore, Alim defines *rapping* as "the aesthetic placement of verbal rhymes over musical beats" (Alim 2004: 388). Rap music developed on the streets of the Bronx and Harlem in the early 1970s. On street parties, DJs supplied the music while an MC (Master of Ceremonies) provided "rhythmically syncopated spoken vocals" (Borthwick 2004: 157). One after the other, the other three pillars of Hip Hop developed on the streets of New York City. Early rappers received the inspiration for their lyrics in their immediate environment. One can say that they were highly influenced by the economic and political changes in the inner city, such as de-industrialization, globalization and the rise of the New Right. The problems that arose for the poor black underclass in the inner city are often depicted in rap lyrics. Central themes in rap lyrics were poverty, problems with the family, conflicts with the law and the state, etc. While rap lyrics dealt with real problems in the beginning of its history (*reality rap*), it turned to more fantastic topics. The main goal was to escape from the streets by dreaming of wealth and fame.

In the late 80s and early 90s, a form of rap called *gangsta rap* evolved. It is important to know what it is, as all three artists analyzed in this paper rap in "gangsta style". Gangsta rap had an "edgy, noisy sound" (Bogdanov et al. 2003: viii), meaning that it is more aggressive and more dynamic than earlier rap styles. Most of the lyrics deal with urban crime, such as drug dealing, pandering or robbery. In some cases, the lyrics are highly exaggerated and do not correspond to the real world. Explicit lyrics and controversial topics are used to attract attention from the media. Accordingly, gangsta rap has often been accused of promoting crime. Anyway, this strategy works as gangsta rap is the most commercially successful form of Hip Hop.

Coming to the significance of rap and Hip Hop in Africa American culture, one can say that they have their roots in African American oral tradition and African folk music. During the time of slavery, slaves had special ways to communicate with each other, e.g. they used drums to communicate messages between themselves. As soon as the slaveholders got to know about this, they forbid the use of drums. Since then, African (American) rhythms are considered to be a protest against the white American society. Rap continues this development by commenting on the inequalities within the society. Rose says that rap music and African American culture go together, as it "is a black cultural expression that prioritizes black voices from the margins of an urban America" (1994: 2-3).

However, there still is the question what the relationship between AAVE and the language of rap is. As Hip Hop is rooted in African American culture, one might think that the language that is used in Hip Hop is AAVE. This not the complete truth. It surely adopted almost all its grammar from AAVE, but there are some aspects that need to be kept in mind. For instance, "users of hip-hop language tend to be members of certain social groups, while AAE users spread across all demographic groups throughout the United States" (Amberg 2009: 155). Moreover, AAVE exists since ages, whereas Hip Hop language does so only since the eighties. Hip Hop language is also used only in certain contexts, such as DJing, MCing or dancing (see also Amberg 2009: 155). H. Samy Alim found an example in which the syntax of Hip Hop language (or "Hip Hop Nation Language", how he calls it) and AAVE do not correspond. This is the case with invariant *be* before noun phrases (e.g. "Dr. Dre be the name"), which is found quite often in Hip Hop lyrics, whereas it is hardly noted in "conversation-based AAVE studies" (Alim 2004: 387). Furthermore, Hip Hop language is far more innovative than AAVE. New words are invented in song lyrics, which are then adopted into AAVE everyday speech. Rapper E-40, for example, is one of the biggest innovators in the Hip Hop show business. He came up with expressions such as *communicator* (meaning "cell phone") or *to underdig*, which basically means "to understand" (cf. Alim 2004: 397). These words then found their

12

way into everyday language of AAVE speakers and Hip Hop fans. All in all, we can say that Hip Hop language can be seen as a subordinated area of AAVE.

2.4 The Research Question

This last section of the theoretical part deals with the research question that is going to be answered in this thesis. As we have seen, there are some strong connections between AAVE and Hip Hop, as Hip Hop originates in African American culture. In order to examine the influence of AAVE on Hip Hop music, I want to find out how the copula is used by African Americans in Rap music. This tells us in how far the use of copula deletion of the three different artists Tupac, Jay-Z and 50 Cent differs from each other. Moreover, it is possible that one artist unconsciously changed his use of the copula from one album to the other. To prove all those assumptions, a linguistic analysis will be conducted in the next section.

3. Materials and Method

In this part of the thesis, the material and method used for the linguistic analysis in the following chapter is explained. At first, the three artists to be analyzed are presented, followed by an explanation of the song selection. The last section deals with the method of how the copula deletion is counted or not. One encounters remarks in the literature that it is not always easy to account for the method. The last section is concerned with the question of which is the best method to use for the analysis done in this thesis paper.

3.1 The Artists

In this section, the three artists are be presented. It is crucial to know who they are, and who they were in the beginning of their careers. The information taken to present this section is all taken from Bogdanov (2003).

Tupac Amaru Shakur, better known as 2pac, was born as son of two Black Panther members in New York City. After the father left the family, the mother moved with him and his sister from one city to the other. They were very poor, but Shakur managed to get an acceptance from the Baltimore School of Arts, which helped him to live his creative side. In 1991, he released his first album *2pacalypse Now* and played a role in a movie. After the release of his second album in 1993, Tupac was an established artist in the Hip Hop world of America. Although he was very successful and earned a lot of money, he began to have serious problems with the law. He was arrested several times and had to sit in jail when his third album was published. Tupac became a martyr of the Hip Hop business when he was shot in September 1996 in Las Vegas. The murderer was never found. As Tupac influenced a whole generation of Hip Hop and got famous through his unsolved murder, he is an excellent candidate to look at his language.

Shawn Carter, or simply Jay-Z, is the second richest rapper in the world and sells one number one hit album after the other since his debut in 1996. Born and raised in Brooklyn, New York City, Jay-Z had to grew up without a father, as he left the family when Carter was a kid. As a teen, he began "hustling", meaning to make illegal deals on the street to make money. Very soon he realized that rapping was all he wanted and created the label Roc-A-Fella Records with two of his friends. This is quite unusual because most young artists prefer a huge label as a jump start. He released his first album *Reasonable Doubt* in 1996. Since then, he came up with one album every year and every one of it being a huge success. With his third album, *Vol. 2: Hard Knock Life* (1998), Jay-Z completed the shift from gangsta rap to pop-rap, which is a far more commercial, lucrative and melodic form of rap. The media say that Jay-Z allegedly raps freestyle when recording his albums, meaning that he never writes down his raps. This unbelievable skill and his talent to market himself made him to what he is now: one of the most successful rappers in the world. Jay-Z is not a rapper only, but also a businessman. He used to be the Chief Executive Officer of the record Label *Def Jam* and owns the fashion company *Rocawear*.

Last but not least, Curtis Jackson, better known as 50 Cent, is going to be presented. Born and raised in Southside Jamaica, Queens, New York City, Jackson had a lot of "obstacles throughout his young yet remarkably dramatic life before becoming in early 2003 the most-discussed figure in rap" (Bogdanov et al. 2003: 172). His mother passed away when he was eight, and a bit later his father left them at Curtis' grandparents' place. As a teenager, he began selling crack, a very lucrative business in the mid-nineties. After being arrested for drug dealing, Jackson started to concentrate on rap instead. Before releasing his first, though unofficial, album *Power of Dollar* in 2000, 50 Cent got stabbed in front of his recording studio in New York. Only a short time later, he was shot nine times and survived. Jackson's story attracted so much attention that Eminem and Dr. Dre, two major rappers and producers in the business, decided to work with him. His official debut album *Get Rich or Die Tryin'* is "probably one of the most hyped debut album by a rap artist in a decade" (Bogdanov et al. 2003: 173). His fifth studio album is going to be released this year. Jackson even started a movie career by his first movie *Get Rich or Die Tryin'* (2005), in which he plays himself. In addition, 50 Cent started a business career as well. Today, his firm *G Unit* markets clothes, ring tones, computer games and dime novels. We can assume that nowadays, he makes more money with his business than with his music.

3.2 The Song Selection

In the next section, the song selection for the analysis is going to be presented. To form a corpus that is big enough to be representative for copula deletion, I decided to analyze two complete albums each from the three artists. I picked the first and the last CD because this gives me the ability to make diachronic statements, as an artist might change the frequency of deleting *be* in his lyrics.

Sources for the analysis of Tupac's music were *2pacalypse Now* (1991) and *The Don Killuminati: The 7 Day Theory* (1996). Please note that Tupac's last album was published under the pseudonym *Makaveli*, and not under his "official" pseudonym 2pac. Furthermore it is necessary to know that *The Don Killuminati: The 7 Day Theory* was the last album that Tupac recorded as a living human being. He died before the release, and the album was published two months after his death. Further music that was published postmortem is ignored in this analysis. Songs for the analysis of Jay-Z's lyrics were taken from *Reasonable Doubt* (1996) and *The Blueprint 3* (2009). *Get Rich or Die Tryin'* (2003) and *Before I self destruct* (2009) were the two albums taken from 50 Cent. Although his first album was *Power of the Dollar* (2000), it should not be identified as his first album as it was unofficially released. *Get Rich or Die Tryin'* was his first commercial success and this is the reason why it appears as his first album here.

3.3 The Method

In the last section of this part of the thesis, I am going to explain the method I used to conduct the study. First, I will mention which instances of the copula are going to be counted in the following study. Afterwards I will discuss the different calculations on the copula deletion.

One issue for the study of the copula is that there is no agreement among scholars which cases of the copula to count and which ones not to count. Blake summarized the different opinions (cf. Blake 1997), building up her own guide on which cases are to count. Blake's guide is the one going to be used in the subsequent analysis, as it seems to be the most appropriate one. I am going to summarize the C forms (= "count" forms) of the copula, followed by the DC cases (= "don't count").

Are, as the second person plural and singular form, was almost always included in the studies investigated by Blake and will be counted in this study as well. One case on which researchers did not agree on is the PS case, meaning variants of *is* with preceding *s* (e.g. *This('s) what they think*). According to Blake, this case should be included as she does not find a valid counterargument that speaks against it. There is no obstacle that keeps us from distinguishing this sound from another one, as we will see in further cases. The next case going to be counted is *ain't*. The problem with *ain't* is that it is not sure whether the copula *be* is inherent in the form *ain't* or not. As some researchers were unsure about it being a copula or not, they excluded it from their studies as a precaution. Blake argued that it cannot be a copula-free item because of its history. *Ain't* came from *am not*, which then developed to *amn't* and further to *ann't*. As a last stage of the development, *ain't* came into being. For this reason, ain't is going to be included and will count for the full forms.

Cases that are not counted in the analysis are those, for example, which are never deleted by AAVE speakers. This is the case when the copula is in the past (e.g. *He was at the train station*), when we encounter *be* as an invariant or habitual form (e.g. *You got to be kidding me*), when it occurs in clause-final position (e.g. *He is taller than the girl is*) or when the copula has the form of *am*, which speakers normally do not delete. Neither do we count cases in which the copula is emphasized (e.g. *He really IS a genius*) because a contraction and deletion of this use is impossible. Forms with existential *there*, such as in *There's those people*, are also not included as they are "nearly categorical contracted" (Blake 1997: 65) and for this reason one might argue that this form does not carry a copula. Furthermore, we find phonological neutralizations when *is* or *are* are followed by *s* or *r*. It is simply not possible to hear the difference between *He's sick* and *He sick* or between *You're right* and *You right*, which is why these cases should be excluded. Moreover, WIT cases, meaning variants of *what, it* and *that* will not be taken into consideration because the last letter of the three words – the *t* - tends to be categorical deleted in case the copula follows. Examples might be *Tha's my daughter* or *Wha's your age again?*. At last, it is important that questions are also excluded because the "flip-flop rule" applies to the forming of questions in AAVE, which means that an inversion between takes placed, as in "*Why you don't like him?*" (Blake 1997: 67). The right sentence would be *Why don't you like him?*. A summary of the C and DC cases is found in table 1 in the appendix. Note that this guide is the one used in this analysis.

Since we know which cases to count and which not to count, the tabulations should be made clear. The first issue researchers do not agree upon is the question whether *is* and *are* should be treated as one variable or not. In the former case, the statistics on the copula do not distinguish between *is* and *are*. In the other case, the absences are counted and shown separately to be able to recognize how often each variant of *to be* is left out. Rickford (1999) found out that *is* and *are* behave similarly enough to be treated as one variable. For this reason I am not going to separate my computation between *is* and *are*. The other issue is concerned with the question of how frequencies of contraction and deletion should be computed. There are two ways to compute the rate of contractions and the rate of deletions each. For the computations of contraction, we can choose between the *Straight Contraction* and the *Labov Contraction*:

$$\frac{C}{F + C + D} \qquad \frac{C + D}{F + C + D} \qquad \begin{array}{l} F = \text{Full} \\ C = \text{Contracted} \\ D = \text{Deleted} \end{array}$$

Both formulae tell us how often we find a contracted form in proportion to all instances of the copula, but the *Labov Contraction* includes the fact "that AAVE could only delete where contraction was possible and that every deleted copula had prior contraction in its history" (Rickford 1999: 64). Rickford also included this fact in his computation of the deletion. These are the two computations for the deletion, *Straight Deletion* (3) and *Labov Deletion* (4):

$$\frac{D}{F + C + D} \qquad \frac{D}{C + D}$$

Because of the fact that Labov's formula makes more sense as it includes the aspect that deletion is not possible without a contracted form before, I will use "the most commonly followed computation formulae in the literature to date – Labov Contraction and Deletion" (Rickford 1999: 67). It is also important to mention that the frequencies shown in the analysis part are always differentiated into contracted and deleted forms of the copula. Counting the two forms allows to get a greater

18

insight in how the copula is used. The more important reason for considering both deleted and contracted forms is that they are linked to each other, as Rickford already pointed out. All contracted forms could possibly be a deleted form and vice versa. The full forms are not shown because you can use them in every position.

In general, it is crucial to remark that changes in the method always change the results. For this reason, the results should not be regarded as the only possible ones. There are ways to come to different results. Also, I would like to say that artists featured on the album are not going to be included, as we only want to find out about the language of Tupac, Jay-Z and 50 Cent. Furthermore, I will also include spoken speech, as rappers tend to say a few words before beginning with their actual rap. Moreover, I will not count repetitions of a copula deletion when it is, for example, in the chorus of the song and thus repeated very often throughout the song. This is the case in 50 Cent's *What up gangsta?* from his first album, whose chorus only counts as one instance of copula deletion. Another general remark I would like to make is that the primary source for my study are the recordings, not the printed text. It is important to state that the written lyrics are merely used to support what I heard to make the lyrics better understandable. All lyrics were taken from ohhla.com, one of the most extensive hip hop lyrics archives that exist. The database is updated every day, and thus, I consider this source to be the most accurate and helpful one for my analysis.

4. Results and Discussion

The fourth part of this thesis is going to present and discuss the results. The results are presented in tables and percentages. In the second part, the results are going to be discussed, finally answering the question how far the results can be an appropriate measure for the copula use in AAVE.

4.1 Results

This section presents the results of my analysis. The percentages shown in the tables were all computed using the Labov Contraction and Labov Deletion.

The first table displays the overall frequencies of deletion and contraction of the copula by the three artists:

	Deletion	Number of instan-ces counted (deleted cases/all cases)	Contraction	Number of instan-ces counted (contracted cases/all cases)
Tupac	57,3%	102/178	58,9%	178/302
Jay-Z	65,0%	89/137	47,9%	137/286
50 Cent	73,0%	162/222	57,4%	222/387

Table 2: Overall deletion and contraction of *is/are* by artist

At first sight, the rates of copula absence do not seem very similar. The lowest rate (57.3 %) is found in Tupac's speech. The second highest rate can be found in Jay-Z's speech, as the copula was absent in 65 % of all possible cases.

50 Cent has the highest rate of copula absence, since he deleted the copula in 73 % of all possible instances. Tupac was the first one to start his career, then Jay-Z followed and the last one was 50 Cent. Thus, we can observe that the later the three rappers started his career, the higher are his rates of copula absence. We will gather additional support for this thesis after looking at the other tables. Concerning contractions, one can say that Tupac's and 50 Cent's rates are almost identical. Jay-Z's rate is about 10 % lower. More or less half of all possible cases are contracted by

20

the artists. The following three tables show the frequencies of the copula of every album. In the first one, Tupac's albums are shown:

	Deletion	Number of instances counted (deleted cases/ all cases)	Contraction	Number of instances counted (contracted cases/ all cases)
2pacalypse Now (1991)	36,3%	29/80	53,7%	80/149
The Don Killuminati (1996)	74,5%	73/98	64,1%	98/153

Table 3: Deletion and contraction of *is/are* in Tupac's lyrics

There is a higher discrepancy between the deletion rates in the case of Tupac. With regard to the copula deletion, the second album has a much higher rate. In 1991, when Tupac created his first album *2pacalypse Now*, only 36.3 % of all possible cases were deleted. Only five years later, when his last album produced before his death was published, the rate rose to 74.5 %, which is a remarkable increase of about 40 %. We can deduce from this that Tupac changed his usage of the copula over time by increasing the usage of deleted forms. Having a look at the percentages of copula contraction, we encounter an increase as well, though it is only by 10 %. The percentages in the table gain greater value by analyzing the percentages of the next artists, as we get to compare the rates. The next table displays the deletion and contraction rates in Jay-Z's music:

	Deletion	Number of instances counted (deleted cases/ all cases)	Contraction	Number of instances counted (contracted cases/ all cases)
Reasonable doubt (1996)	55,1%	27/49	40,8%	49/120
The Blueprint 3 (2009)	70,5%	62/88	53,0%	88/166

Table 4: Deletion and contraction of *is/are* in Jay-Z's lyrics

In 1996, when Jay-Z's first album came out, he deleted the copula in 55.1 % of all possible instances. Thirteen years later, he had a higher rate of 70.5 %. Thus, there is an increase in copula deletion of about 15 %. In comparison to Tupac's increase of 40 %, this increase is far less intensive. Another factor that has to be mentioned at this point is that there are different time intervals between the first and the last album. Tupac made his 40 % increase in the time of 5 years, while it took Jay-Z thirteen years to make a 15 % increase. We can deduce from this that Tupac's speech got more "vernacular" faster than Jay-Z's one. In the end, they both have the same copula deletion rate of about 70 % in their last album. In the case of copula contraction, there is a recognizable increase of about 12 %. Thus, it is almost as high as the contraction rate in Tupac's first album.

All in all, we can see that Tupac's and Jay-Z's use of copula deletion and contraction show similarities. In both cases, there is an increase in the usage of copula deletion, so that in their last album, they both have similar deletion rates. Nevertheless, Tupac enhanced his usage of the AAVE feature faster than Jay-Z did if you have a look at these two records only. Concerning the contraction rates, there is the same increase recognizable in both artists' speech.

Finally, we are going to have a look on 50 Cent's development of the copula use:

	Deletion	Number of instances counted (deleted cases/ all cases)	Contraction	Number of instances counted (contracted cases/ all cases)
Get rich or die tryin (2003)	80,8%	105/130	56,8%	130/229
Before I self destruct (2009)	62,0%	57/92	58,2%	92/158

Table 5: Deletion and contraction of *is/are* in 50 Cent's lyrics

Concerning the deletion rates of 50 Cent, we have a very high rate of 80.8 % in his first 2003 album. Six years later, the rate decreased by one fifth. Out of the three artists analyzed, 50 Cent was the only one that lowered his usage of copula deletion. One has to keep in mind that he had a comparatively high rate in 2003, meaning that his speech was very vernacular with regard to the usage of copula deletion. His average rate of deletion is with 73 % the highest of all three artists (cf. Table 1), despite a lowering from the first to the newest record. Having a look at the

22

contraction rates, there is only a 1.4 % increase, so that almost nothing changed in 50 Cent's use of contractions.

The next table illustrates the six analyzed album according to the decade in which they were published. Three of the records were published in the 90s, i.e. the two by Tupac and Jay-Z's *Reasonable doubt*. The newest Jay-Z record and both by 50 Cent were published between 2003 and 2009, thus in the next decade. This is shown in the following table:

	Deletion	Number of instances counted (deleted cases/ all cases)	Contraction	Number of instances counted (contracted cases/ all cases)
90s	56,8%	129/227	53,8%	227/422
Since 2000	72,3%	224/310	56,1%	310/553

Table 6: Deletion and contraction of *is/are* in different decades

In the 90s, the rappers chose copula deletion in about 57 % of all possible instances, whereas after the millennium, they did so in about 72 % of all possible cases. There is an increase in copula deletion of 15.5 % from one decade to the other. This means that the three rappers increased their use of copula deletion and therefore developed a language that is more vernacular compared to the 90s (at least concerning these two albums that were analyzed by each of them). Concerning the usage of copula contraction, there are no significant changes. The rate rose only by 2.3 % from the 90s to the next decade. We can therefore conclude that no further interest in contraction should be made here, as there are no significant changes in the music analyzed here.

4.2 Discussion

In this section I will summarize the findings and discuss the question how far the results are valid and can be seen as representative of the copula use in AAVE.

The analysis has shown that contraction is more or less the same in every artist's speech because there are no significant changes in the rappers' language concerning copula contraction. All we can say up to this point is that contraction is used in about 55 % of all possible cases (cf. Table 1). The statistics also show that contraction does not behave commensurately to deletion. They do not depend on each other on the first sight, but we have to keep in mind that the formula of copula deletion already involves the fact that deletion can only take place when contraction is possible as well. According to Labov, copula deletion depends on copula contraction, which is why he used another formula as other researchers to compute the rates. Considering all rates found in this thesis, one can easily recognize that the contraction rates did not change significantly over the years, whereas the rates of copula deletion did so. Having a look at the rates of copula deletion, it is striking that they fluctuate because the discrepancies between some albums are high, e.g. Tupac increased his copula deletion by 40 % from his first to last album. The contraction rates behave more similarly, i.e. they do not fluctuate as much as the deletion rates.

Coming back to the results of copula deletion, one observes that both Tupac and Jay-Z increased their use of copula deletion. They both have higher deletion frequencies in the newest album than in the first one. 50 Cent forms an exception, as he was the only one who had lower frequencies of copula deletion in his last album. This observation gives rise to the question why an artist lowers or increases the use of vernacular features in his language. The sociocultural aspect that changed by first being poor and criminal and then being rich and famous plays an important role at this point. After becoming a rap superstar in 2003, 50 Cent did not hang out "on the streets" anymore, but lives in a huge mansion. The people he deals with are not drug dealers anymore, but highly-educated people (e.g. working at the record label or lawyers) or other people and artists who do not necessarily talk "street talk". There are not so many street hustlers or gangsters around him anymore, who talk a low class language. As the environment influences how we speak and what we do, we can assume that this social factor might have changed 50 Cent's use of copula deletion. This statement gives rise to the question why there was an increase in the cases of the two other artists, as the lifestyle of Tupac and Jay-Z changed as well. In the Hip Hop world, there is the assumption that every artist should be "real" and "from the street", meaning that you should be authentic and never change who you are or forget where you come from. Talking as much vernacular as possible might be a way to stay "real". As Hip Hop is a very popular music genre, especially in the

United States, being as "real" as possible might attract more and more fans. This might have been a reason for Tupac and Jay-Z to boost their copula deletion rates on purpose.

Concerning the call for authenticity, one should not forget that those rappers are never really the same person that they were before the commercial success. They do not live in the same "hood" anymore, do not deal with criminals anymore, but are rich now. It is hard to believe that this does not change the personality and further the language of a person. This aspect has can be helpful to explain why a rapper should a high influence on the language of the three artists analyzed in this thesis and thus plays an important factor on how the fluctuations of the copula deletion can be explained. Another observation that can be made is that rappers developed a more vernacular language in the course of time. Comparing the rates of copula deletion of the 90s with those after 2000, one easily sees that an increase took place.

After having made these observations about Tupac's, 50 Cent's and Jay-Z's use of copula deletion, there still remains the question whether the results of the preceding analysis can be rated. Can Hip Hop music really be a reliable source of AAVE language use? One aspect that is obvious is that almost all rappers use the AAVE dialect to communicate with others and therefore use this language in their music, too. One problem we encounter here is that music is creative. Our language use is not the same in music than in natural speech. In the following, several examples will be shown to illustrate the difference between language in conversations and in music. The first aspect to be mentioned is that we rarely find full sentences in rap lyrics because constructions with the gerund are used quite often. As we deal with a gerund construction, there is no subject of the sentence either. An example might be the following lines from Tupac's song "Toss it up" (cf. *The Don Killuminati*):

> Lookin for suckers cause you similar
> Pretendin to be hard, oh my God, check your temperature
> Screamin Compton, but you can't return, you ain't heard

In this example we can recognize the above mentioned issue because the artists does not use the full sentences, such as "I am/you are lookin for suckers cause you similar; you are pretendin to be hard, oh my God, check your temperature; We are / they are screaming Crompton, but you can't return, you ain't heard". By applying gerund constructions, Tupac avoids using the full sentences, making it harder for researchers to measure the real appearance of copula use in music because you would not use as many gerund constructions in conversational speech. This does not mirror the actual AAVE speech, as the gerund is part of the artistic expression in rap music.

The next issue is concerned with rhythm. As Hip Hop is a highly rhythmic music genre which depends on the beat, there might have been cases in the preceding analysis where a full form of the copula was deleted because the lacking of this little syllable better fits the beat and the rhyme scheme. There might have also been cases in which it is the other way round, meaning that you would use a full or a contracted form to fill a gap in your lyrics. Another striking aspect was the speed of the music. One easily recognizes that when the beats per minute are less, the rapper raps more slowly and thus tends to articulate words more exactly and therefore has a higher potential to use full forms. This does not correlate to the normal language use of AAVE either, as the words you choose do not depend on your speed or rhythm to speak in formal language. In music, it does so, as we deal with a colloquial form of speech. The next issue encountered during the analysis deals with style. Due to stylistic reasons, certain constructions were repeated, such as in the chorus of 50 Cent's *Wanksta* (in *Get rich or die tryin'*):

> You said you a gangsta
> But you neva pop nuttin'
> You said you a wanksta
> And you need to stop frontin'
> You go to the dealership
> But you neva cop nuttin'
> You been hustlin a long tyme
> And you ain't got nuttin

In this chorus, we find the rhetorical device called anaphora, which means that every (in this case) second line begins with the same word. The first and third lines are even almost identical except for one word. There is copula deletion as well. In "natural" talk or writing, we would have found only rarely a construction such as this one.

Due to all these issue we encounter when analyzing AAVE in music, we can deduce from this that music is not the best source for AAVE analysis, though one should keep in mind that it remains a source, as AAVE is often spoken in Hip Hop.

5. Conclusion

All in all, the analysis conducted in this thesis gave a quick insight in how often copula deletion is used in AAVE in music. It also showed the different frequencies of copula deletion. We do not only find differences among the three artists. There are also variances and similarities that manifest themselves over the course of time, e.g. the rappers analyzed in this thesis paper tend to apply copula deletion more often the later they started their career, at least concerning the two album of every artist that were used. These finding should not be generalized, as we deal with a short, exemplary analysis. Moreover, we also need to state why it is of major interest to have analyzed AAVE in music. It is interesting to have a look at AAVE features in Hip Hop, as this music genre is one of the most popular music genres in the United States and in Europe. As so many people listen to rap lyrics, Hip Hop music is the only medium in which people really listen to the AAVE dialect. Not everybody has a neighbor or friends speaking this dialect. Another possible outcome of this thesis is the finding that AAVE in music is not necessarily the same that it is in spoken speech. The artistic value of music in general gives rise to the assumption that there are grammatical constructions that are more often or less often used in music. Thus, music can be a good source, but it is not necessarily a good one. Nevertheless, the analysis conducted in this thesis paper showed an example of how research on AAVE in music can be made.

Abbreviations

AAVE – African American Vernacular English

SAE – Standard American English

AAE – African American English

Works Cited

Alim, H. Samy (2004). "Hip Hop Nation Language" *Language in the USA: Themes for the Twenty-first Century*. Eds. Edward Finegan and John R. Rickford. Cambridge: Cambridge University Press. 387-409.

Amberg, Julie S. and Deborah J. Vause (2009). *American English: History, Structure, and Usage*. New York: Cambridge University Press.

Baugh, John (1983). *Black Street Speech: Its History, Structure, and Survival*. Austin: University of Texas Press.

Blake, Renée (1997). "Defining the envelope of linguistic variation: The case of 'don't count' forms in the copula analysis of African American Vernacular English." *Language Variation and Change* 9:57-79.

Bogdanov, Vladimir, Chris Woodstra, Stephen Thomas Erlewine and John Bush, eds. (2003). *All Music Guide to Hip-Hop: The Definitive Guide to Rap and Hip-Hop*. San Francisco: Backbeat Books.

Borthwick, Stuart and Ron Moy (2004). *Popular Music Genres: An Introduction*. Edinburgh: Edinburgh University Press.

Green, Lisa (2002). *African American English: A Linguistic Introduction*. New York City: Cambridge University Press.

Green, Lisa (2004). "African American English" *Language in the USA: Themes for the Twenty-first Century*. Eds. Edward Finegan and John R. Rickford. Cambridge: Cambridge University Press. 76-91.

Holmes, Janet (2008). *An Introduction to Sociolinguistics* [1992]. Harlow, UK: Person Longman.

Labov, William (1998). "Coexistent systems in African American Vernacular English." *African-American English: Structure, History, and Use*. Eds. Salikoko S. Mufwene, John R. Rickford, Guy Bailey, and John Baugh. London: Routledge. 110-153.

Rickford, John R. (1999). African American Vernacular English: Features, Evolution, Educational Implications. Malden, MA: Blackwell Publishers Inc.

Rose, Tricia (1994). Black Noise: Rap Music and Black Culture in Contemporary America. Middleton, NH: Weslyan University Press.

Tottie, Gunnel (2002). *An Introduction to American English*. Malden, MA: Blackwell Publishers.

Winford, Donald (1998). "On the Origins of African American Vernacular English – a Creolist Perspective, Part II: The Features." *Diachronica* 15: 99-154.

Wolfram, Walt and Erik R. Thomas (2002). *The Development of African American English*. Malden, MA: Blackwell Publishers.

Wolfram, Walt and Natalie Schilling-Estes (2006). *American English: Dialects and Variation* [1998]. Malden, MA: Blackwell Publishing.

Wolfram, Walt (2008). "Urban African American Vernacular English: Morphology and Syntax." *Varieties of English: The Americas and the Caribbean*. Ed. Edgar Schneider. Berlin: Mouton de Gruyter. 510-533.

<u>Appendix</u>

Table 1 Source: Blake 1997: 60

TABLE 1. *Potential DC cases in studies of the copula in AAVE and related varieties*

	Cases Researchers Agree on					Cases Researchers Disagree on							
	Past	CF	Emp	Be	Are	Dey's	PS	FS	FR	Q	Am	WIT	Ain't
Labov et al. (1968) (NYC)	DC	DC	DC	DC	DC	DC	DC	C	C	C	DC	DC	DC
Wolfram (1969) (Detroit)	DC	DC	DC	DC	C	C	C	DC	DC	TAGS	DC	DC	?
Bailey & Maynor (1985) (East Texas)	DC	DC	C	C	C	C	DC	DC	C	C	C*	C	DC
Poplack & Sankoff (1987) (Samaná)	DC	DC	DC	DC	C	C	C	DC	C	MISC	C	C	?
Rickford et al. (1991) (EPA)	DC	DC	DC	DC	C	DC	DC	DC	DC	C	DC	DC	DC (+NEGS)
Winford (1992) (Trinidadian Creole)	DC	DC	DC	DC	C	C	?C	DC^b	C?	C	C	C*	DC
Blake's Guide	DC	DC	DC	DC	C	DC	C	DC	DC	DC	DC	DC	C

^a Instances of *am* are included in Bailey and Maynor's calculations, but they are tabulated separately from *is* and *are*.

^b Winford excluded these tokens when making comparisons with AAVE.

^c Winford (1992:31) noted that, "In accordance with the usual practice, indeterminate instances ... were excluded from the analysis." This can easily be deduced for the instances of CF because all of the previous researchers exclude these cases. However, because researchers disagree on whether to include PS and FR cases in their copula analysis, it is unclear how Winford evaluated these cases.

Key:

Past = past tense forms of the copula (e.g., *I was small; If we wasn't playin' now.*)

CF = clause-final copula (e.g., *He is better than the girls Ø.*)

Emp = emphatic or stressed copula (e.g., *He IS an expert.*)

Be = finite and habitual *be* (e.g., *You got to be good!* (imperative); *Each year he will be gettin' worse* (modal); *His wife is suppos'a be gettin' money* (infinitive); *I see them children [who] sometimes be down yonder* (habitual))

Are = all forms of *are* (Ø, *'re*, *are*) (e.g., *We Ø ('re) on tape.*)

Dey's = form of *is* with existential *there* (e.g., *There's these poles.*)

PS = variants of *is* with preceding *s* (e.g., *This('s) what they say.*)

FS = variants of *is* with following *s* (e.g., *She('s) sixteen.*)

FR = variants of *r* with following *r* (e.g., *Your('re) right.*)

Am = all forms of *am* (Ø, *'m*, *am*) (e.g., *I'm tired.*)

WIT = variants of *what, it,* and *that* (e.g., *It's a real light yellow color: Tha's my daily routine; Wha's your name again?*)

Q = questions (yes/no, wh-, embedded) (e.g., *What are you doing?/What you are doing?*)

Ain't = the negative form *ain't* (e.g., *They ain't but so big.*)

33